© 2006 Robert Allen
First Edition
All drawings by Luc Paradis

Library and Archives Canada Cataloguing in Publication
Allen, Robert, 1946-
        The Encantadas / Robert Allen.
Poems.
ISBN 1-894994-17-5
        I. Title.
PS8551.L5556E53 2006   C811'.54   C2006-903205-X

Dépot Legal, Bibliothèque nationale du Québec
Printed in Canada on 100% recycled, ancient rainforest friendly paper.

CONUNDRUM PRESS
PO Box 55003, CSP Fairmount, Montreal, Quebec, H2T 3E2, Canada
conpress@ican.net   www.conundrumpress.com

conundrum press acknowledges the financial assistance of the Canada Council for the Arts
toward their publishing program.

Canada Council   Conseil des Arts
for the Arts   du Canada

The Encantadas
Robert Allen

All nature is so full, that that produces the most variety that is most examined.

– Gilbert White, *The Natural History of Selbourne*

*I am afflicted with the sense of how many whom I have known are dead,
and how little evidence I have that I myself have lived what I remember.*

– Wallace Stegner, *Wolf Willow*

I
Jack

1

... snow striated, shiny as baleen ... last in a closed loop
of graveyard notes; jots, glosses on this or that scrutably
sad self. The gulf admits no other. Well, either

these notes or his own sweet self will survive; betting windows
still open. When he writes, he feels fine, fine. Looking
up, he surveys what lies beyond the window, bellying

world as full as a sail, beyond sloped shingles; through
glass so old it's flowed into its own boots. He writes
in the gravebook: *march equinox, winds westerly & cold.* (He'd

2

heard Melville wrote *Moby Dick* holed up a winter, daydreaming
leviathan up over the sill and into his book.) No simple voyager
of now and here would acknowledge the place he's beached: stark

spruce, cedar; old purple rocks with hats of cloud; yet a jungle
three months from now, greenly tangled, then red and yellow,
falling into fall; and he, here, reworking it all: clean

blues and blacks on a white folio; dream swept of webs
in its darkest corners. No shadow there at all, though he writes
of a shadow of shadows, with all his bright skill. He might have been

3

a week old again, come to sense his newborn self blinking
in a new world, awful and separate. Strange now that death
must brush against his coat before he learns

fully that living is something done apart
from artfulness, that solo in his skull shell / frailest
of craft / he has no craft to help him. He had drifted

in the whaleboat too many days and nights to count,
wishing not the slightest breaker to rise
from the flat blue sea. Now he is lying here, yearning

4

for event, peaks in a brainscan; from a coma at last shaken
loose; at last, a living, thinking man.
                                         Cantons de l'est —
Strange, the evocations, when he writes this. Avalon, Eden,

The Hesperides; not homely home, but home of the first
humans, or of half-human gods. He lines up a knothole in the barn
with the falling evening star, nearly gone as it drops

plum into the sun. Its cool mildness was a lie, as it ever was;
an inferno of wind and fire; lifeless, they're certain now. Once
like arid Mars, it teemed with biots and comic book rovers. / Here

again. Far from the sea, seasons unstable and violent as
they pick up and move on; storms pull a five-foot swell through
dry corn, not yet ploughed under; thunder and lightning

bang their way through the Little Magog Valley; spring
floods on which tight New England style houses unaccountably won't
float, but launch their sailors from high windows, on cushions

and boards. Fronts, squalls – spells, the sailors called them –
come on us in a blinking like the furies from hell, having whirled
up close under hill cover. Broken horizons

make a fractal jumble, fair places to hide. Thinking on it now,
there's really no comparison to the sea's open face; there, you can
see the hammer falling; here, weather hugs the hillcurve, over

well-worn paths; it is human, treacherous, domestic. Then it can
rise like a madman at the opera, high hat and cape, masked
face with its smile. Fixed. Singing with the violence of the sea,

until clear sea weather. *winds westerly & cold.*

                                                     Stuck on that.
He's left reverie like a stamp on the afternoon, puzzling this
landscape, left a dozen years before for the sea; then he'd come

home, going meadow to meadow, tree to tree, like a kitten making
its curious way back, to a shape more than a memory, via
empty fields, unscribbled meadows. May Second when he'd

climbed the stairs to the back bedroom, sat on the sagging
bed. Same blue & white checked quilt. Looking past the windowseat
at green candles of grass, burning with controlled haste, as if

for him, through the last dirty corn snow in the ditches, in
the shade of leaving trees. And in the first breath he took
the hills went summer-green; elms darkened, picking the teeth

of the gnashing sky, then slashed clouds open
with green umbrellas. And when things had burned
greenly for a while, they became red coals, then ash. With

the slightest of shifts (time becomes numbers) they were
gnarled and black again; and on November Twenty-third (duly noted
in the book) snow fell overnight and stayed.

                                        Part ghost,

part man, he blinked his eye and the windows changed,
summing up the whole furniture of childhood: he was as
much parcel of all this as the maple woods, the family of

9

foxes that owned the high pasture – once mowed and open
when the farm was working, impenetrable now, but for sparrows
and partridge. He'd even seen, floating from one

dark spruce to the next, a snowy owl, and noted he'd
seen it. December Fifteenth, 1963. His father and he once trapped
one, accidentally, in the shed. It became tame, feeding

on mice and swallows in the hayloft. Too tame – Red
the Airedale (later dead himself by misadventure) bit off
its head, trying to make it play. / The years seem, now

10

he brings them forcefully to mind, like a collection
of lurid book jackets seen through plastic covers, waking him
at the age of ten or so to the shaggy dog tales

of sex and mortality. The mortal sense grew in him
in time to follow the last measured months of his father's breath,
dying away in a genetic foul-up as inherently funny as a fat man

falling down a long flight of stairs. No use to inveigh, once
the tumble starts, against the cruel edge of each step and riser, or
the malign comedian who put them there. Fifty-four now (then?)

he's worn that reflex so deeply in, he can only mark fall or loss
with the observation that he, himself, in his dad's words, seems fine so
far, shipshape and Bristol fashion; much as his abandoned god must

tire quickly of the flocks of particular sparrows, falling too fast
to count or care; finally with an earthquake of a shrug to bless
the lot, R.I.P. where they lie; or like the winter sparrow

in one window out the other, back into the storm, a warmth
briefly given, then darkness fore and aft. (Archie the owl
loved sparrows too; when he swallowed one headfirst, his eyes grew

12

impenetrably dark.) Years on, Jack became an
oceanographer, because you cannot freefall through land; and of those twelve
years at sea, enough said, for now. He picked up a pen, wrote a poem

of coming home: *Land's a silent listener; siren as familiar / as the theft
of consciousness each night in the blue & / white quilt. I fell
from the blind / fragrance of half-sleep to dreaming. Maple*

*boughs, thicker / and greater in number now than when I was home
before, / tap their black knuckles against / the ancient glass....
Wilder now, but still / the same measures.*

He can feel the edge

of the farm, the hills, the river snaking through wetlands, losing
itself in many channels before losing itself in the lake for good. Twilight
a blue creel full of old fish scales, an ocean pared

to bone. Beyond a thousand iterations of all this, the sea; a childhood
sea, blue, deep and endless; not the lunchbucket sea that was his work,
but a sea whose azulado nectars he thought he could breathe,

like a fish; where a finflick could put you in coral courtyards; a sea
to song & dance you of wild evils, always on the brink of winning, and
always, in the nick of time, foiled. Back home, the too-familiar

14

offer cold hands. They reach down from the sleeper's port, so
the galleon dreams are tethered, and you awake where
the voyage began, older and unmoved. / A third of life: twelve

years sailing the main, only to be brought home, a wounded
conquistador, from death's dooryard in the blue Mariana Deeps.
Working on salvage, he'd hardly stopped to try the old sea on

for size – working so long with tanks, compressors, deadlines – all
at once he was five years old again, in the moments before sleep. He sank
so slowly; sank from blue to black. The sea was warm above him, a quilt

of sun. He thought he could reach down a thousand feet. When
he bumped bottom, playful dolphins knocked on his nose....
Brought instead to his own dooryard, he awoke in a strange

familiar room; green; peaceful as a sea from which squalls have
vanished; to which, now, pelicans, clumsy as first love, swoop, folding
long wings, topheavy beaks open to gulp sunshine. So tired.

A tenth straight day diving for a galleon's treasures. Why
had he done it? He was not the kind to want the sea to rock him
in her arms. But he had felt light, careless, full of pointless

16

fun. He made faces at fish; danced slow with eight-armed suitors.
The very upside-downness of the sea struck him as absurd, and proper.
So right he'd taken out his mouthpiece, laughed with recognition.

He didn't know what it was he was abandoning. For a while
he thought he was in an aquarium. He spent four days on a ship
to Manilla, dozing, half-dead, a lovely feeling. Only he got

better and better and it started to hurt. Through a porthole he watched
cupric seas, swelling with a bellyful of things, things he couldn't
quite get close enough to name. He longed to clamber out to name them.

17

There was an owl in his room. There was a woman there too. She was
amnesiac. Gleams of recognition came and went, sun
on whitecaps. Once he stayed awake long enough to write the

word *delirious*, and the relief was as if he had spelled all the names
in the world. Apparently he asked the nurse for mice. He feared
the ship was an old slatted barn, full of holes, and would sink.

Later to San Diego by navy jet; a civilian plane to Chicago; vivid
half-memories of a glass palace. He talked with Miss Wisconsin, 1983,
on a train to Toronto. Her eyes acquired depth suddenly. The world

was 3D. He walked with a cane, up and down stairs. He was
at Mirabel, then endlessly in cars, until a kind friend assured him
he was home, that it was May. He watched a flight of geese headed

north. The familiar V. They were blind, stupid, going home. The sky
raged with a spring storm. Sometimes the sun stared with a single bright
eye. Swift clouds followed one another, towing blue, far-off.

Write it all down, suggested a helpful doctor, writing himself, a string
of prescriptions for various drugs. I felt the muse run her fingers
lightly over my lips. *I took the drugs. Kiss me, muse; kiss the doctor,*

then go. / Snow becomes rain on the attic window. A heart beats
beneath the roof. / He tilts his head under the mothballed quilt, inhaling
naphthalene; all motley, scraps of garments and sheets, like the

mixing and reissue of genes. They have all fallen behind
the slope, the great-grandmothers last to be seen, clearer
in his mother's mind than his. Just one elastic consciousness;

inside, the world must fit; swollen cell; one tatter in a sail.
Alone in a room full of boxes and bicycles; shawls, trunks,
teddybears; lugged, one and all, to a still

heaven at the end of change. No place other for them than
this posing, infinite in photographs. Dusty heroes; expatriates
from first floor wars, bumped to the dusty crowsnest

of his mother's house. / I feel similarly placed here, ready
to get into the clothes of my old self, go downstairs into her
good graces. Beyond the flimsy sheets of window glass, bellying

into the world, the sheared crops of my dead father's fields, crow-
haunted poplars now. Winter made a shantytown, staying
here, sheds more akimbo, derelict objects that used to be

working parts of a farm; leaves sodden, blocking drains; bedroll
in the ditch, tin cans, Molson bottles – a table picked clean of all but
rinds and scraps. Muse, you should not have stayed the winter.

You're a harridan bound with twilight stays, jutting your hips like
a cheap date. Paint fading, you sashay the sky, dignified despite
the lack of art. Go and sleep in your bone-grey boudoir.

Now there's only Death to stare down, all fawn-unblinking, come
from my watery grave. He's losing interest, slowly, has not looked up
from the Sunday Times crossword in hours. I want to drape his

scrimshaw shoulders in something other than sky. While he stays, I
tell my mother, *He's our guest.* / St. Stephen's Day. / On the steep slope
of ancestry he squalled his first. As Dawkins said, there are few

ancestors and many descendants. On this incline, his father, had
not, then had, blown himself out; all matter had not rolled like a ballbearing
down time to becalming. What must be the nostalgia

of his mother for his father? A theatre of light and dark curtains,
though the light source is extinguished. / It was a jolt seeing her: such
carving on her face, as if an old seaman had done it. Grey hair, tangled

and long. Death had distinguished her, that most slick and lounging
of lovers, the same as waltzed, St. Stephen's afternoon, in different guise,
no doubt. A white cockteaser. When his mother reached the barn, the dance

was over. As if taking breath old Jack had lain his flesh vessel
on the hay. She'd lain there with him, on the edge of understanding, hardly
daring to cross on to this new plane alone. His wide eyes mirrored

old snowfields with the rot of corn beneath; her own seasons, or
theirs together. A naked dance partner appeared to take her hand, light
and strong, as a snare twirling a snagged rabbit high. When she looked

on his comfort in the hay, no backward look at all
could she coax from him. *Death*, his face reluctantly adjudged.
His eyes looked like they had never lived. Though

she could make him whirl and die, over and over, kissed
by The Snow Queen, his ghost rubbed against her, goaded, coaxed
and swore. No further would he go. And no further

would she. A while later, she rose from the rick
as from sleep, roused by the rattle of a pick-up
down the mile-long lane off Katevale Road. St. Stephen's

Day, 1970.... / He knew her first letter to him by heart: *I think of nothing but Jack, Jack the father and the son....* It had been him in the pickup, he thought, at the wheel of a '53 Merc, assembled

of rusted parts stored ten years in the barn. Uncle Bob's truck before he disappeared from sight, one mist-wisped morning, five minutes after sunrise, late August, no year.

Oddly, he himself had come home in a half-ton, same colour, though newer. Same maker – Ford. (Enough to make a man religious.) He was half conscious, but fully aware, sea-

daft. What surprised his mother, lifting him from the cab, was
the picture of his father he'd become, now that time had filled in
some of the thicker strokes. A solid week, he'd raved

on the salvage tug, Mariposa, claiming his father was
his next of kin. His mother heard the name, Jack, just
the name. She'd last been postcarded five or more

years back, a card from the Galapagos, showing
The Isles of Ash, turtles and parrots inset, old Darwin's
finches incandescing the slag. / I can't travel the reef right side up,

the rapture overwhelms me. Riven to splinters of free
laughter by the notion of coming up, for air, lunch, redemption
or a lucrative career, I float merely; float over coral; watch useless

varieties of fish shape water as a knife shapes soft stone. And as
I drift, I think, I am out of everything. I am out of crimson lips
to kiss, and butter, eggs, sirloin and milk.

The day the card arrived, it was as if, now, parrots and finches
flew through her own apple trees, as if for the first time she saw
her world in colours; grief for husband and son slid

down an incline, dropped over the horizon. Doors and gates yawned
open. She'd sharpened her heart on absence. It cut now like clouds across
the silk sky. For the first time since his going, she invited ghosts

into the kitchen to sit, eyed them as possibilities. / He had
no notion. There passed a year; he lay on coral, little boy on a scarlet
blanket, watching bubbles rise from his mouth, array themselves

like stormclouds in the current, as so many mornings he saw clouds
tear up atop Mount Orford, bound east, with shrouds and shreds
of old weather. His mouth closed and opened, compelling bubbles that

cracked like eggs four hundred feet above him, each (he imagined)
fat with its own singular speech. Laughter passed; sadness winked, brief
as a butterfly; unconsciousness followed: a hundred hours in one

long winging, the sea-flight of hummingbirds. Not for two months at home
did he remember breaking into air. An undoubted fork of yellow lightning
struck the barn, blew a five-foot length of two-by-four

through the only pane of glass not boarded. He hit surface
in heavy swells, warm wind-twisted tunnels of rain. Sky
tumbled by him in blue pieces. He slid down long fallopians

of light, Sunday school beams from the fingers of God, only
in this instance shafted down from bony thunderheads, bruise-
blue and erectile. He felt in no awe of the stormy Pacific, just

euphoric and light. He might well rise to his feet, follow those
lightshafts home. (The German couple at Uxmal; whose daughter
taught English in Montreal. The man came as close to tears

as a German could. Then Jack realized he'd got the tense wrong.
She was dead and he was thinking of home.)
                                        He came in from
the barn, shaking, went to the wicker chest full of games

and toys. History said, "Here's a quick costume change." (A lot of things
are talking to him now.) It has an elaborate front, is backless, is held by
elastic fasteners. He dances to the room at the top of zigzag stairs – a ziggurat..

So now a black top hat, tapdance routine, cane and all. A Rops erotic
walk along the walls, *La Dame au Cauchon*. Downstairs, dinner bones
petrify on plates; on blackened pine chairs, bony diners rise

from dining, licking bone chops with bone tongues – his mother's
baked ham was something special: glazed with honey, rosy with life; pantheons
of yams, carrots, potatoes; homely roots, anointed with red-eye gravy. It's a far

cry from Hotel de Gobernador dinners: mangoes and papayas, the morning's
fresh concoction of rum and juices; raw fish delicacies, incised into a kind of
Japanese inscription. Chilean wine, white and chill, at least a couple

bottles worth. Blue Mountain coffee. All taken on a limitless veranda, white,
its own horizon, on the shade side of the hotel, moving as the sun moved. Watching
white sails flaw the sky, mist build across the blue as night draws on. Until,

after three cups of coffee the sun has gone; then it would pour rain for
an hour – he, meanwhile, moving into the bar to talk to the same half dozen
men and intricately replaceable women. All of these, too, mysteriously

severed from bygone times, as he was.

                                    When the truck, sideslipping,
rattling down still-frozen lane ruts, turned the last bend, his mother
stood guarding the inner gate, eyes weaponless. Locally, freezing

rain scored the tin roofs, stung his hand on the door panel. Four
miles off, Orford reared into a paradisal blue; clearing always begins
west, and the mountain wore a blue and ragged scarf; sunshafts

broke on some meadows, tall grasses lit like ranks of iridescent
feathers (sunset in the grey land often being gaudy as parrots). Still
dressed for the funeral? No, but a smart navy-blue ensemble; younger,

and better turned out than he'd proposed to his homing self. She met him
halfway. They about carried each other to the east porch, skirted in grimy
snow, shaded by three new spruce, grown

to maturity in his absence, planted (he thought he recalled) by
his father in 1960, that afternoon Mazeroski hit the home run
that beat the Yankees. (On the kitchen radio. Staying home from school.)

They replaced a golden willow, circa 1850, taken in a winter storm in '58, burned
as firewood to stave off a dozen others. That willow wood would burn for hours,
though dead at the heart, leaving an ash that ran through your fingers like time, and

35

a fragrant, lingering smoke. They were retracing the path his father had
taken to the barn, feeling maybe the first hot warpings of his sight here, face
silky smooth against the air, feet planting left, right, left, right; as they'd

been taught; cold, cold – his body unflexed, unused. Awkward, sensible
of earth, four thousand miles to zero G, lips tingling, abstractly poised
to laugh, carol, kiss, address the mysteries. All his senses agreed, he was

fast turning into a wooden doll, deftly painted with grin and apple cheeks,
but fragrantly dead as the willow. One leg tried to step too far; half his face
went sullen, the other half smiling at the joke. So he sat in the barn, just

within the door, rested his head against a stall, good eye measuring
the clouds, moving calm as ever past the narrow gap between the door
frame and the half-closed door.... (Do I believe the sum of my

account? Some of my account — so help me, I gave up ends for means
when I first put words on paper. So: what better knell than owlcry, the
owlcry sum unreckoned, sounding from the blue; loosestrife that

summer climbed the stair of wind, a blaze along the lane where
he looked, made notations of the gnarling, measured tree-growth
with the one eye, thinking, I think, of how a living tree and a dying

tree are inseparable until you have looked for half your life. / Now take
my own submersion: half-dozing in blue-bright, I sank into the deep.
Hearing nothing. The heart beat on. Small plosives of sugar and oxygen,

depth charges. Nothing in the lizard brain rebelled. Nothing tried
to wake me, though I thought I glimpsed the soul, oblate with pressure,
ascend in a white bubble crown (up the down staircase which I

descended). Later they diagnosed narcosis, told me I'd no right to be so
unconnectedly happy. But even then I don't think I'd lost my knack of weighing
one state against another, not even shot up with narcotics.

What's that

clatter downstairs? My mother stacking dishes, doing things calm
and purposeful, whistling light operatic airs. Outside, a passel of ragged
crows ragged-crowing, I can see them sail low through the scotch pines

to the roadside, more distantly across the meadows, dark specks criss-
crossing lazily. In our long winters they speak of spring, as gulls around
the mast-head speak of land. At least I have made landfall, still

falling, though slower, much slower than before. Don't think of the meadow
as golden grass, but as uneven stubble shot through with slate outcroppings,
cliffs along one side, dark slag. Which Isle of Ash is this? Snow

uncovers it, apparently bereft of life. Sodden hammocks; the bones
of fences; winter's viscera. / Downstairs in crow-dark nearly, early
light starts to saint our eyes. I ask her why she's down so early. She

talks, but I don't make out words, only grey sounds like gravewindings.
Has she even been to bed? Sunlight rises up all around suddenly, as on
the gilt helmets of the islands' discoverers, sad to the soul

to find no gold, for which they have a sick longing. No one discovered
here. Tribes crossed it to get from one place to another, Iroquois
and Abenaki. / Later, the house is adrift on summer seas. Jack's

home, I tell the crows. True-blue Telemachus, or Swee'pea maybe,
balmy with depth sickness, becoming myth in his own telling ... (Like his
father, embalmed in a night a whole lot longer than voyaging. Waxing

deader than the dead of night. Becalmed) ... so much so that when he comes
to the lip of hell to lick the black blood, it's mostly a kind of philosophical
talk, like dead heroes exchange: And so, what brought you here...?

Miles beneath his breath he both acts and narrates. Somewhere he's
read: *These are poems you could write in your sleep.* The dead Jack wears
at least three suits, keeps a clothes-rack in history, boater

and cane, for his rare appearances; he always exits solus, smiling; a distant
and loony crescent of forgotten teeth, harder porcelain than his other matter.
Left scattered at home in an invisible softshoe; and the whisper: this will

be you.
                    Meantime, knitted up
from the same proteins, coded to tears and laughter alike, Jack hears
his mother's half of history; eyewhites shot

red, cheeks pale and faded as the quilt, he propped against
the headboard in full view of the plume-tailed weather vane, pointed
south at border hills dropping, stony, dark-timbered, into

Vermont. She's paused, and curiously assessed his eyes; tucks
her hand under his, gaunt, limber and seeming without bones. "It's
alright, darling. You've been asleep a long time. You're

home." She'd kept the attic alive to just that possibility,
mounting the stairs with longing eyes each morning – this
she told him in the very room – arranging bears and dolls

in wicker chairs, against pillows. The Jack she'd
wanted back? Not the sailor, deep-sixed, but Jack the tar
of pond shallows. Middle-aged, unshaven, as soft as tallow,

43

he burned with the fever of years on an alien main. What was he now?
A featherless biped, huffing yellow sheets full of breathsong – scents
of the long-made bed become, in a few days, alive again. In her

eyes, he guessed, he was lying as still as his father in the hay, snow
a crystal shroud, unmelted on sallow cheeks; pinch-nosed thin, a dissolving
snowman. Jack, who snored like his father had; born gift

of a scything angel. Oh no, snow won't melt on his tongue (dreamy
smile for my mother; lights lowered, first row) eyes
at bottom of shafts, winking at the star Sirius: as if priests, in some

inner chamber, had flung open the closed doors, for
sun to sweep the altar clear, immaculate still down ruined
centuries. / As Dzibalchen, he recalled then, hacked

out of the jungle weeks before he'd gone there, a week
free (and a Spanish guidebook, fifteen pesos in Corozol) so he could
sit smoking home-rolled cigarettes on a lately reconquered

doorsill; sit and will a green tideflow back; a Mayan Canute.
The jungle spat flowers and leaves into dark doorways; snakes
mounted vine ladders up the stone sides; to indian star gods

45

as alien as the Southern Cross. He pretended he was the only
Mayan left; up and gone, his brothers and sisters, sifting from
known Mexico; half-picked meals left for the rats and crows,

masonry scattered like children's blocks, as much as seven miles
from the site. X marks nothing, as the jungle knows. I rest
my stony head upon my knee; my bones darken like coal. I lay

me down in the limestone dust; no still or turvy water anywhere.
I rest my hand on crumbled palaces, ground myself against its shoal.
Why here? Why should I be here?
                                        Buzzards of death emerge

from town in a black and chrome Chrysler, disembark, three of them, to view
the corpse, a silky parade to the barn to fetch him. / "Ma'am, by gosh, he's stiff
as a barnboard." / A litter unfolds, of aluminum and canvas, leaned, while

they palaver, against the shed, next to barrow, shovel, rake, clayed boots, now
tokens of the dead, to be burned or buried with him. / "You got some shoes
we can put on him, Ma'am?" / They exit like conquistadors, circumspectly eyeing

my father's gold teeth. These are the only things that might be beaten
into new shape, the only malleable thing they will pour from the hard porcelain
cups of his teeth; no maggot can sup on these.

                                         The guidebook waxes: The great

Mayan civilization turned stony and alone; stand in this doorframe, gringo,
have an exotic camera capture your breath. Or in the gift shop you may
buy it ready-made.... (My translation.)

So, one muggy afternoon in

The Late Cenozoic Age (it was Bastille Day, I think, and the year may
have been 1981. It was shortly after this my own breath bled out in the sea.
The sun stared like a basilisk, making a sunny chop. I was not diving

this morning, but waiting for the tide to turn. That would fix it at around
four, and the slant of light then always made things tricky. The Santo Cristoforo,
my boat, twice the size of the little craft I would use later

to smuggle wine into England. / She is Dionisia, and rots somewhere in
a coast guard shed.)

So he went to sleep in Mexico, woke up in Katevale, one
bright and neverending morning full of drab choristers; vireos whining

the same note over and over from the eaves; *sweet sweet sweet* of half
a dozen song sparrows tumbling in the lilacs; chickadees, surplus
from winter; warbled song from beyond the pond; maybe the great

grandchildren of the orioles: first breeding pair he'd noted this far north,
August, 1970 – two weeks before sailing in the old red Mercury pickup
for Galveston, he thought for good. / The world has since changed by

more than orioles: a mock-up self now hops through a sea of hay-flecked
sunshine in the barn, so leaky between boards it's full day inside; a yearling
heron back on the birthpond; he takes a few headers down straw-

strewn ramps and steps, thrashing at webs and flailing at disuse;
flying off the handle (he loses his temper at nothing) sometimes led
by heart, sometimes by head, because, say, the junkman

adjourned with some childhood treasure, or swallows shat
on the eighth-grade world map carved on pineboard, where it
sat atop split shingles, two-by-fours, dented eavestroughs, odd-angled

saw scatter; thus an old world in deep shit, while the sea
sounder mapped a new.

                Counting conscious minutes on his fingers, he
measures his father's lands in a gimpy, rolling seawalk, shoulders

unevenly falling and rising. Twelve years gone? His bubbled breath
infinitely condensed? By now he is gravid with unbroadcast light; a white
hole. Not to have got word to his mother, all those years – then

when he did (one time) not to have alluded to his father's
death at all. Narcosis anyhow has freed him from that burden, now
that he doesn't live anywhere.   anymore.   but a bright

sea without current, overwhelmingly larger than guilt, a dizzy
bubbly ginger drink he takes in like a big cartoon kid; waves rolling
metal-hard on a long stone beach. During the dive he had almost

loved the loss, about to be separate from himself, a state much
like sleeping. He met the light more than half-way. Its weight grew
light as a hummingbird, hovering near him in the current, earth

dropped like a lead plumb, away, leaving only a feathery medium
light as cream. Now he takes the map and adds to it with a felt
tip: *here be whales and monsters of the sea.* Then a whale-spout filigree.

And thinks of Updike's words later, on Nabokov: *paradise wherever*
he alighted. Full fathom still, below the naming: *Mare Pacifica, Golfo de Mexico, Mare*
de Sol ... it's confusing: up on the high brass bed his insides boil

from the elevation. All the world's seas lie beneath him like a scattering
of coins. At World's Edge (he can now see that far) red cherub cheeks
puff, blowing him beyond names. (That's not quite true, it's just a romance.)

On blue untroubled surfaces, life goes on, a coat of paint
obscuring the dark underside: sirens with summer mouths, begging
him back down, to sleep on the tilted galleon again, the boat

perched on a coral crag like a party hat, green algae shrouds caught
in the rigging, flapping in the flow, for all the world
like sails. / Something hailed him, he knew not what: Katevale

hills unfurled. Mars fell on his head, but the rest of the world
was beyond knowing: down a dark path to the midnight river, lit
by stars and only stars. The old world swells like a corpse,

the old world won't light, like a sodden lighter. (But your finger
points flame at me, flares into daylike brightness. After I will search
your lips in darkness: the whole river of you, once stepped in.)

So I must move by morning. Where? Travel-mad, summer-smitten.
A flood is in my eyes, en epic. I must go like Gilgamesh, still an undrowned
hero, through an air full of tail-flickings, engulfings, blind carnivores; through sky-

borne weeds that loop and shimmer. The gravebook ends in commonplace:
noting bare temperatures, wind direction, fronts, cloud types. Somewhere
were poems in which I rose like a golden urchin, right and rich in words.

But moving in space is what I do best, what I do now. The whole
air of earth can be thought of as a sea, to move side to side, up and
down, back and forward in. / & half on purpose he fell in, circled once,

55

was gone....
              & here the story becomes a whisper; listeners rise &
head off into night. Emblematic Jack who sprang among them
lies with a stake through his heart, lies buried at the cross-

roads. Where the gravebook went is anybody's guess — lost
in a green-flecked tension on the river maybe, while at the dead
crosshairs a bodiless child lies, playing its own slim, invisible

legbone, like a flute. (Legend has the child leaping
adroitly into a woman's womb, falling like a feather to stick
there, a playdart or cocklebur, spirit latching on to flesh

like the *feu follet* trapped in a jackknife, or the tyrant from Genesis
caught flatfooted in a carpenter's son.) Gnostics and Jews
for Jesus are making a revival. No saucer has come for us, as we

get set for chaos, a president's heartbeat short of the millennium,
smoking sweetgrass or dope to see straight. The last time a thousand
years rolled over midnight there was dire news, more

psychosis than usual. No second coming. How long to breathe
the pure air of exile, here in another's country? In one answer
life ends inside a billion years. Many will still be looking. / In

fourteen hundred and ninety-two, Columbus sailed the ocean blue – do you
see him springing from the serpent's teeth you sowed? Yes, you. Are you
happy up there in the top hat of America? Can you sail clear

of the white, ice-jammed straits, find shade from a predatory
sun? / One morning I awoke at the crosshairs of a dream,
ascending a green beanstalk into a land of solid cloud. Child-

hood things lay strewn everywhere, a chicken laying opal eggs, a steam
train sadly chugging, the ruins of a petrol station, nosed by a three-wheeled Cooper
in British Racing Green. Some giant kid was bawling

his eyes out, unwanted and unborn. He held the disconsolate snapshots, the saddest
you've ever seen – they did him for a family. We floated on, day on day, paddling a
reed boat with our hands, riding a winged horse.

Only much later when he cried into my hands did I see he was me.
I let the sun in just a crack

                         – and where was I? On the wide veranda
of the Hotel Gobernador, on the brink of the wide, blue sea....

Here, darkling, the end of the road, your happy
grin tallow to seal the century, your meerschaum head
cast on a grey beach; your life on the Isles

II
The Antedeluvian Vaudevillian

59

of Ash / – come & gone, gone & come; talk is of Atlantis, a fat lying tongue.
Apostrophe – You won't get to Hollywood, Ted. To the bisque bred, you'll find
we eat our young and our successes, parade them in scandal sheets, before

and after they're dead. / GALAPAGOS TURTLE GIVES BIRTH
TO ELVIS'S HEAD / MIA & WOODY SACRIFICE YOUNGEST CHILD
IN SATANIC RITE / ALIEN WROTE DYLAN'S LYRICS / MAN

SNEEZES AND EYES POP OUT / NEW HUBBY FOR LIZ?
Galapagos Ted – yes, that same lounge lizard implied
in the oceanic tryst! First amphibian in Eden! Out of the blue! God shakes

his fist, whacks off his own head with a scimitar. The shell game! (not Elvis at
all, though the slicked-back hair, centre-parted, brings Rudy Vallee to mind) ... singing
just for you, jacktars, at the Hotel Gobernador, with complimentary

prawn cocktails for all, outside beneath the apricot moon – but Ted's
running off with himself. He always does, snoozing half up
the beach, evolution's untimely etched box leaking its secrets. Secrets! He cannot

run swiftly like the hare, cut through the air like a swallow,
swashbuckle like Flynn or dance like Astaire. *Only poor flesh
in a gilded pot / Teddy's my name and I like it a lot* – "Ladies

61

and Gentleman, the Hotel Gobernador is proud to present, straight from The Isles
of Ash where he danced out of his egg! That heavenly hoofer and
heartthrob — no, friends — no empty shell or hollow Armani suit — the Antediluvian

Vaudevillian, the one ... the only ... Grandview Ted!

                                               Gringo, drifting
the length of beach as you drifted the world's length. Shells lie everywhere, yellow
and pink inside, whorled and opalescent, winding to the point of nothing

where storms from the ocean, like songs from a single note, rise to cloud
the sun. Shell beaches are rare on the Galapagos, where Beelzebub's
own black moat rings everything with ash. *Las Encantadas*: the enchanted

lands. Drifting islands shift, restless outlaws, kept from
harm's way by a tidal intelligence sensed by its first sailors; their
charts were useless, since the islands sidestepped every voyager

who aimed his glass at them. Ted wrote them as tapdancing
turtles in the show he staged for them, so they'd sing
songs of loss at sea to the Broadway carriage trade – till given

the vaudeville shepherd's hook the minute they tapdanced
on the maps. Get lost, lost islands, is Ted's song, heading for New York.
In fact they will get lost with him, each a map of the other, a blue-edged,

63

tear-dewed map. So the bestiary starts, imaginary animals
with tides both in and out, following Ted's score. / "The map has gone, how can we
grow old, grandma's tears have made the barbecue cold...."

Mazurkas of suitability, sonnets of survival, dead-end elegies for some. Our
turtle Ted doesn't know where he is in the litany, hanging on the breast
of the moon goddess, all growed up, floating in the tide grass singing hymns

learned from the boy bands, buoyed by the salt to near divinity. But the lot
of the ardent shell-clad amphibian ain't what it's cracked up
to be — not given his dreams of the legitimate stage, and a new canny fear

of oblivion. Clack! Clack! It's the new lost carol of turtles coupling, like
the sleek heavy machinery, yellow diesel cats, brought to eat the islands
down to their roots, never mind the lacelike shimmy of new life

in the pond. Clack! Clack! Our engines are warm, but we will refrain
from coitus as it curbs our desire to colonize. Say bud, this place will look nice con-
do-ized! We'll truck in sand, fence off a safe stretch of beach, machine

gun the guerrillas, put bank machines by every king-sized bed, kiss
our fingers while we grind our heels, dance our dance for you, while we transform
jungles to malls, your raw germ to our own kind; while indians, savages,

communists, tapdancing turtles with stagestruck eyes, the long ladder of creatures
climbing out of the sea, all give way to the thousand year real estate reich. CONDOS
UBER ALLES, writes a PR snake. / Exit Ted, up right / pursued by cream pies. (Follow

Ted's adventures in succeeding numbers) ADVERTISEMENT / and now some *sturm
und drang*: bridge to chorus, more of us each geometric progress: Ted ain't
sure why slow thinking so resolutely saddens, as in a walk through the garden, taking

eons to complete. Fabulous feather'd gizmo swung on a string,
dragged through the sky, precursor to Ted's amphibian fear of flying, his
dream nightly of face-slapping fronds greenly careening while

Ted's hand on the joystick guides him through the atmosphere.
Sunk in a slew, hung in the lightly raised fist of gravity, lunching
through the feathery inviolate creations born to be lunch –

not so obvious, the chef's latest creation, a cheesecake sculpted
to look like waving orange tails skipping in unison along the reef – sky
gets dreamily turned with the rear-left lateral flick of a claw, the mouth

absorbing one-celled things like kisses. The difference between
sea and air is obvious to one who's been there open-eyed. Sea has
a weird middle distance, a weight like a hologram made

of nothing but light, photons piling in the viscous wash of Ted's
flow, more subtle than the ripple & wrinkle of a dinosaur's approach
in water, not so clubfooted & Jurassic. Ah, a dancer's life. And if

he should dream of Humboldt Saskatchewan or Passaic New Jersey,
it's by grace of books; he's swum under the lighthouse, to the volcano, by
the still waters, over the bounding main. He's still a foetus rolled

up in his own eyes – there's self-awareness for you
in a land where unconsciousness is king. His own heartbeat, wired
to a monitor, dooms him forever to idly count: one two

three, one two three: the small tides a second apart, moony
pulse of his own salt seas inside, fast and deadly. Oh, to turn
turtle and eat mud, to settle in silt, to trace the body, heartless

in the silicates, to lie down and grieve once and for all for eater
and the ate! Alden Nowlan's elephant had the world for a shithouse
and Yeats pinned love to the place of excrement, where the donkey tail

of it could be yanked by children, not yet mortal or sane.
(... new bright day, Seventeenth of May. Jack from his box pried
locks and vaulted. Jackyboy mastered flight with the faultless

assurance of the man in *The Golden Ass*. Grasswidowed mother
deep in a book – sucking on the gene he got it from, a candy of
codes, black hieroglyphic scribble, his doom ... trilliums unfolding

in the thickening green grass; frogs piping, hot to heave their bodies
at anybody's blood, bloody homeboys strutting copulas and blues
riffs, metering out the song of life that is precious as folded wings

on one imputed angel on pinhead patrol, scarf slung with Fokker
daring, goggle-eyed in spring, mock-mad as the singer in pastoral
measuring his horny heart on old glockenspiel time. Jack's friends

are mostly women, timing their blood to simultaneity.
All in accord they laugh, invent crazy and crazier cocktails. And all
his friends are exes of someone, hurting invisibly, as only

the conscious can. So he starts singing softly, *All My Exes Live
in Texas* ...) Now let's count the stories: Dionysus paddling north
with wine from Crete; Daphne turning with the leaf's turn. Viking endearments

at the door: hwaet! wassup? Ted prayed for a simpler age: more derring-do
& less Derrida. Paid no mind to the text, just loved the unrolled scroll
of hill; saw god not, but degodded nature. Wrote poems, dedicated

verses to Anne in suitcases under the bed, to Ruth who called this
work in progress *The Enchiladas*. It's hard for Jack and Ted to share
a cliff-edge house too small for two to write in, share a body

and a voice. So, Jack: in a dooryard with the barn as horizon; with toys
in the mud as event; with the sword hand hung loose down the right
thigh, with a dead dog chasing its live tail in the one damn

Polaroid left turning pale with the ghosts of the preterite – no
cupless handles like commas reminding him to quaff his drug in the lief
silence ... count off: teal, telos, tortilla, tortuga – an Indo-European

counting game seems to sound from the damned left speaker
of the TV, a documentary, Odysseus sailing home to Ithaca. He got there
in a mere ten years, chugging along through the Aegean. But

got there, slew the zootsuits, then crewed his barque westward
to death's knell, after a few happy years with Olive and Swee'pea.
Or is that another story I got wrong, adrift on the winedark sea...?

So, Ted: Ted's favourite century is the fourteenth, with black
death, the kid's crusade, like that minivan nightmare to Disneyworld,
and of course the rivers that ran blood of the *Jacquerie*, before

Marx, before the industrial age, stripmines & the longhaired mer-
maid, Mia Farrow, in *Payton Place*, and the outmoded myths rejigged
into sitcoms. Maynard & Dobie, The Skipper & Gilligan, Ethel & Julius, Ethel

& Fred. In Ted's clutch the eternal wrangle: who's the best dancer,
O'Connor, Kelly, Astaire – or Ginger who did it all backwards on high
heels? They rode the warm stream to Greenland before anything got

settled, losing touch, brother from sister, in the viny Sargasso. Not
one in a hundred makes it back to the New World, but Ted did. Out of rapture.
In their multitudes they had childhood stories, while the one left becomes

a myth /

III
Body with a Mind of its Own

One Day long in the past, Jack, he'd followed a sweet bridge
of Utah juniper through a gunsight pass, down to the Cimarron
Valley, where inscriptions marked the spot some Libyan travellers

had perished. Drank a thermos of hot coffee and watched
a rattlesnake forked and killed by brown-skinned indian kids, one
of whom was a blue-eyed Ojibwa from Estevan, Saskatchewan,

(as lost in time as the Libyans), whose father'd helped the Bureau
of Reclamation build the Hoover Dam, where all the water in the world
was hoarded for some future. Then he'd gambled, not so much

with his own future as with his last gallon of gas, in Cactus
Jack's casino, built on sifting dunes. Ozymandias sang
here too, tunes slow and easy in the tart twilight air of caravanserais

here and gone, as stars twinkled immeasurable ridges away,
countless as the grains of sand. Why was it not possible
to be oceanic at home, but just in some monastery of thirsty

windows in Gallup, New Mexico, on old route 66? Though it was once
beneath water, and is still as fragrant as the sea. Coast to coast,
my baby – rocky bones, stiff in the cold deeps, swimming

comes like dinner, a blizzard of delights to choose from, a scissor-
kick back round to face the waiter, all black jacket and white teeth, like
a shark. Lord, he is back on the wide veranda of the Hotel Gobernador,

a dozen years later. And what's changed? The same cryptic regime, the same
hotel letterhead, the same two dozen Pacific shrimp doused in lemon juice
and hot pepper. The same dashed egg of the setting sun, lying

broken in the swell, so blue, then crackled with spilt light, then black
under tropic cloud. More German tourists, noisy as gulls. And of course
his own life, a deeper keel. The sea's a blue-veined skin to be contemplated

and kissed, no longer to fall under, not knowing which way was up. His daughter
wrote from school, "The food's okay, there's a club here called Viola's, full of guys as old
as you, daddy, matching each other shot for shot, and a kind of post-punk band full of

men as old as Keith Richards, skinny as a bunch of dried herbs, and one lead singer who's
a ringer for the young Mick Jagger, like a ripe mango with lips ... could you put a hundred
in my account? The kind of decadence that fits an education like this sure takes CASH!"

Note 1: Bulldozers woke me up this morning. Heat got me down. Got a letter
from Trace. Not a thing to do about anything. Not a worry. Bought some coke.
Eighties drug. (Where did you hide those mushrooms?) Note 2: The woman named

Rosa Diaz who organized the squatters was picked up by the police. Then they
levelled the place; that explains the bulldozers, a strange place to see John Deere green,
though this place runs on long green entirely. They still collect passports

in the hotel, and there are visits from men in 1940s hats, who have watched
many old American movies. Sprinkles of gunfire like salt in the tequila; the back-
taste of salty lemon; the bruised face of the maid when she comes to turn

the sheets at night. Still genteel, in a maid's livery also reminiscent of movie
servants. Still polite. Not she or I will leave this place. It's papers, *señor*, papers.
Meantime our planet drifts in local space. It is well-policed, though most

of the galaxy is free to wander in, if you have the time. Note 3: First ensure
the body's survival, taking food at the edge of the self. Much
madness is ingested with lunch, a BLT or plankton, there's a rule for

this: I yam what I yam, Popeye said, dopey with hope that Olive Oyl
would hold him in the frame of her want, the way a shell holds the snail. Don't
fail to grasp this – wuz I whut I wuz then, holding Polaroids

that wilt like fall flowers in the first frost? Running so fast
in the bowstream of a carnivore makes you appreciate
the boundary. This is me, my attempt to be not the snack

that regulates some body else's blood. Some body else ... now
you're talking. You're you at least in this. Not some maladapted
Dane, or fucked star dribbling life into his mainline. Chemistry

adds you, like your BA, MA, phi beta kappa key. Arm-long
list of accomplishments – but that tiny ticking time bomb in your genes,
sweet phonemes that flower into poems, or unread letters

to a lover, or just some antisocial comment on-air, addressed
to space on a talk show vector. You deserve to be the author of a slow
burn, like the one that levelled Northern Florida, which God

knows was already level enough. The world spins unconcernedly
beneath more selves than is good for us. Us? I drink. I wait. I pleasure
myself while waiting. I write a million drafts, carelessly

breaking the sentence into separate lines, breaking the speech
of my life into manageable bytes. I will not know what you write
back tonight, or tomorrow, most likely. It is precisely 12:40

on a July night. The moon waxed full an hour ago, so if I believed
in astrology, or the Tarot, I might go to sleep with significance
weighing my eyelids down like pennies ... not liquored over with

uncare, but in the supreme illusion of the self, still I lay me down, in
the creaky cradle of my own limbs, to await what tomorrow might
bring, aside from a waning that's like to make me lunatic.

Rain on the tin roof, cosmic dust bursting bright in a deadly
shower among the Perseids. Lives ease in and out of being in such
dereliction, you know God is either long-gone or slumbering,

sunk in his junkie dreams / walking on Ste.-Catherine the other day,
Heather said of a man holding out his cap, "Doesn't he look sad?" Sadder
than the rest for this instant in time, but that's not worth

a thin dime. Fair wind shapes the sea. Fair time, both wave and particle,
pours out like orange crush. Jack tastes its dribble on his chin, tastes
no one he properly knows. Buzzards are back

in the Townships, more than ever since the ice retreated
back to Franklin's bones. Doves too, though they auger no ark, and the one
day wonder of day lilies, planted once but now domestic, rearing

each year as faithfully as milkweed. He's discovered pitcher plants
growing by the creek, gnawing at the sky, thinking to drink the flying things
like a dream of staying high. Once cocaine did that for him, now

the land of Cockaigne, delivered whole with just a little wine, in foil
wineskins, is instantly retrievable through the embroidery of self, this
self which is self-evident, and so demonstrably the rhapsodist. Who

sang the song? The singer. Who wove the hammock he sleeps in? Rain
seems. Song seems. Moon wanes. The world once so vast now is a sentence
and the love he feels for it an old grammarian / my spine feels

like the great divide. We were made vertically symmetrical, two eyes
to see you coming, your face fixed like a shuffled queen of spades. I drove
purposely to the roof of the world, following nothing more than a cart

path along the ridge. All the blueness, the roof of a mouth, a bruised
eye socket, wearing down from the gritty wind that blows three
quarters of the day, dropping an hour into turquoise night, to leave

the cold settling in high hollows. Manhattan could be built again
in the lower stratosphere, pretty as a book cover. But what's the use, it would
wear away faster anyhow, like the top bricks of civilization,

all ground to dust, the petty generals and warlords
perched on it like roaches on the stone feet of Ozymandias. Word-
smiths beat that old song silly. Crooning filled the air off vinyl

wheels. Bix, that last time, pointing the cornet at the Jericho walls, didn't
have a fatal thought in all his bones, but lived high in the melody
for three minutes. Just the time it took to read the notes, hung like

black cataracts. All downhill, downtime. R.I.P. Frank Sinatra, razed just
like The Sands, crapped out – first Zappa, now Sinatra. I'm deep
in the lives of the saints, and a rhapsodist. My ex-wife wrote me: "Jack

I need five hundred, slip it under that rock just at the tip of shadow there
beneath Mount –" She didn't see me under slabs of shadow thrown by Manhattan.
I think, sure, five hundred seems like a drop in the bucket & flag a yellow

cab. I want to reach oblivion tonight, but make it only to 133rd before
my muse corners me, also looking for cash. There was a time she'd do it
for free, now it's money up front, U.S. greenbacks, which she insists

on counting before offering up inspiration in the form of a crimson
mouth. Sing you, I sing you, deeply & only at night. And where does she
go when I lose consciousness? Lose heart? (White

letters on white paper:
she's fucking brilliant and won't
take cheques / eighty-eight

keys on the piano. Eighty-eight keys to losin' the blues. I let
my muse hit me, dropped my guard. Sore ribs are a small price to pay. She can't
hit, slugs like a butterfly, comes full-blown out from cracks like

a silverfish, simpers like a fat fairy godmother on a coach and four
if I come up with so little as one good line, builds sandcastles with me
on the seashore. She sells. Poems on the other hand, especially those

that go on and on, have no buyers but other johns of the written word,
already shuffling off, hands in pockets, ashamed at selling what, so
patently, the universe tonight is full of: feints of starlight, trying to bruise

the whole of a black night, swelling closed the single eye
that flew up high to see it.... From where I now stand, I can see the twinkle
of Las Vegas, and on the other side, the far sheen of Lake Mead,

a fake swimming pool to go with the penthouse view. This thought,
I think, will be my postcard your way.
                                        Interlude: as Montaigne
said, always have your boots on and be ready

to leave. The windows brim with reflections of ghosts dressing
to be gone. That's what living in an old house alone will do; just
cover the walls with those you think you loved; I'll talk

to them awhiles, talk to anything moving. I say, Are you going do you
want to leave do you know where you're going? Sometimes I say we can
make leaving fun. I say when you're twenty what you're leaving is

just dross (wine-dark with hope as she goes out the door) you know you
have an equilibrist's footfall. Light breaks on the steps, nude descending. Look,
I don't want a fullblown nostalgia here (but the fact of leaving implies

the left). Are there any things said or unsaid and do you know you are
leaving the way they always leave in poems, brainless and with a flourish? And
there is what I don't say (and it nearly rhymes) though at the time it always

seems like courage. A gracenote now: when leaving is with words
it can never stop, but will fill everything your life is quiet with, so
no object does not follow the mirror curve of what you thought

to say or thought you said. (If this is too abstract, think of the writer who
died in a room stacked floor to ceiling with papers containing the frozen
contents of his head. But he forgot to account for the lack of readers.)

A lot of people were eyeing the red maple trees. They quickly lost colour
in the squalls that autumn. The mirror emptied. I was thinking of Mr. Soutine.
When I lit out for the west I left an unfinished poem, returned to find it

complete.

      Jack drives to forget himself, but always steers
back into remembering. Without a mind you can only have fun – you
don't *know* you're having fun. With such profusion of blue

highways, it's almost possible to believe in your marrow that the slight
touch prints cleanly, so that memory is a physical thing, and incomplete.
(As Johnny Cash, playing Homer Simpson's recall: "I have no new

information, I'm just your memory.") Messages fly himwards from Mars,
from the blue guitars. Woebegone poems from a lost Welsh bard, trapped down
a mine in Wales. I haven't been back to the place

I was first brought into, so my history's
there for the taking; it talks me in, talks the hills and barrows and rich
peat of my own story.

I wanted more for so long that now I want less, want it cold
as a dog's nose, as a girl's knees, cold as the heart
that wrote the isles. / This

weekend, Eurotrash races around the island
at 213.4 kph as a bubble of rain swells up and rips near
horizontal through the high air, though there's never

more'n a zephyr on the ground. And no known weather in anyone's
south, west or southwest; (Your guess is as good as Jack's. Your
dream might as well be his.) Breakneck

car or blue guitar. Alone or seemly grouped, family is a long
stretch at Sing-Sing: whoever holds your hand is close enough
to reach; whoever pulls herself from

the horizon will walk with you down the beach; and the sea
pulls off with no haste, indolently handling its sing-song watch.
Sand, sea and salty waste; a sly lycanthropy

digs deep through every landfill, subtending
any house. No geography stands still, though there
is a whole ocean prying the bluffs apart. The sea

fills like a rutted driveway, drying through July, and strewn
with hopeful weeds. Narcissus pining in a puddle, face razored
from the muddy map. Tantalus waiting in line to fill a tin cup

with water. Daphne mounting back into her laurel tree, for good
and ever, so scary the modern world, held together by wild TV
stories as real as any myth. The thing about the stories we

remember, so much has been removed, leaving just the bare form,
like blackened timbers tracing a half-burned house. The thing about now
is we know too much, so much it makes us sick ... devils

who've seen too many deaths, angels solus on bloody clouds,
a god who's reminded himself, in the course of another hopeless dream,
that carmine, carnal, charnel, shambles, shit, are all incarnadine. / What

I think now is it's time to shut up, speaking has used up half the night
and I've forgotten who I'm speaking to. When the moon and the sun share
the sky, something bad can happen; when I listen and talk both, a shudder

of light threatens to send the words back into a pit, not strewn with the bones
of other dead speakers, but miniature pathways so small and zinging
with particles, there's no way of walking there. Would you talk

spread out on a white blanket like that? Picnic in that vacant lot? (I am decked
in fine clothes and talking to you. You are naked, as in those Manet outings.
Neither of us can take enough wine in to head off embarrassment,

making love would just be other conversation, too easy because
I am making you up. You say reasonable and smart things, though
my memory clips you off after seven words, like a phone number.

It is frustrating – while I am working, painting you
like Botticelli, you are slyly slipping into Ruebens, with a smile
recondite as silt below fast water. How can I even get the blue

eyes of you not to flow away on a river of forgetfulness. I need
a whole reprogramming, I guess.

                          you make me blue

I have a key
you make
me   aster   blue flag   chicory blue   stained

with the sky you spilt   strained through baleen
clouds   you be
lily for a day   weed-

wacking sun   made to make order
like the fire's sheen
your wicker grin

like sloe gin fizz, corona, lime,
true crime it is   blue cantonment   corrupt as a limehouse villain
night chill   black blood on the sill   parsley

sage   rosemary
spun tumblers made the beastes and fowles and flowres
of the woode   solstice   sun   moon

bars of shadow reach the foot of the capstone
empty pueblo now   Abenaki once crossed
my woods, swiftly fleeing quarrels

of the English & French   send postcards   words
fail   here there & everywhere   hawkweed   milkweed   ox-eyed
daisy   summer came & went   sun a cool yellow   raed

unraed.)

IV
Alarms & Flights

       Ship out, she said, and my muse packed me off. *You need
a break*, she said. My muse sings silver text, but saves the lumps of coal
for me. We were sharing a joint and I thought I had misheard. (I wonder

when I smoke what centres of the brain start to kick in, and out, and when. So
you tell me, what's missing here? The problem with me, I pay too much attention
to attention, can feel the electrochemical jolt like two train trucks banging

together, as one neuron engages the next. And so I miss what's
happening.) She made me get out of the cart and stand on the streamy path, facing
upriver to a height of land. I don't know what the spine of the country, cracking,

said, but a downswivel look brought me to a bay, scything off to cloudy
north, though drunken blue, all sunny chop by the jetty. A newmoon boat sat
tethered there, bow aimed for the Apple Isles. I was older than

always. Grizzled, unshaven. The sun lit me as it did Orpheus, fresh-stepped from
Avernus bright. Must be he thought a bit then, about where his next
step would take him, or even if he would go on standing. Taking to his bed, a rock

as pillow, he couldn't have felt worse about the future than me, having
fucked up big time, craning around to see what he could not let slip
through his fingers, but did, as surely as sunrise. He was no great

traveller after that, tethered there. I felt the same, taking and throwing
the tether down on my familiar grounds. I felt as if I had walked the same
deep path forever, between two poles of the familiar, while the sun

took its path too, invariant, walking off behind cloudy winter, then
walking as surely back, when the snow had melted and the ground was
hard again. Now I stood, unbound, with going not the problem, only

when, how, how long, how far. (Teddy tidebound, house on his back,
slipping in the warm current winding home, programmed to stay in it and
not stray into the colder edges, like Orpheus again, those boundaries

laid down on the road to hell: *thou shalt not shake the apple tree; nor look back across your shoulder; don't reach for me; don't love me any how but how I want you to; take no one but me, & I leave it all up to you....*) The sky

coppered with cold tonight, long-off snow; glittering turquoise stars litter a dusty cummerbund thrown down on the elliptic. All habitable places are there, that's where snowy presciences lurk, proteins tangled up

with godly words, waiting to drift down on the shivering womb of life hereabouts, salty flow of spiral & semantic seaweed, spelling out endless sonnets with just four dice. (Of course, I am just a roadie on

Ted's world tour. How cunning a creature could I be? Shoddy piece
of carnal machinery, metabolizing with a pen stuck in the corner of my mouth,
foolish enough to want to write, beached now & incommunicado ... oh,

it was explained to me. Since god went down there's no getting to the server
& email piles up unsent & unread. The lonely heart can turn to silicon, and will,
before we'll have a clear channel. But the roar of surf in a strong onshore

wind has me up, stumbling to make coffee, waking to the easy
chatter on the docks, sharpsailed fishercraft already tacking out beyond
the bar, & no way of keeping the flame of the stove hot enough

to boil water.)
        When you change intonation, you change
the meaning of the word; when the dark descends on language
the mandarins come to play, niggling

changes, immense fripperies, like the voice of God out of a scroll
inscribed three thousand years ago. There is a soundtrack in the earth,
voices like a solo cello, emerging

from the soil in spring, mindlessly
ebullient; more and more I listen to voices as they are freed,
patting authors on the back as they

107

emerge, fresh frankensteins, new
as a baby's cry. Less and less do voices commandeer me; their harsh
slate language, their newness,

their inscription in the air —
a poem read carelessly, from a book picked up
by chance: likely to steer me

to a new frame, a movie of myself
from year after year; the snapshot afforded by fifty years
on earth, hazy

Polaroid, without author or director,
developed in the air; my director, fashionably
festooned by a baseball cap; my element, the swift

chiming of today; a cloud, obscuring
the sun, temporary, lapidary; snow
falls over tonight; a clear and moonlit

pause after I'm asleep, an hour in duration, and it's dark
again, it's always, on waking, clear and
dark again, and shot with shooting stars, and the shock is I'm so far

from the last dark I started from, so close
to the one on me now. / Atlantic beaches are fine, migrating islands
and bars, one moment encroaching, the next drowning

in expectation. Might as well make a continent here, like potting
a plant. Let's rear up some skyscraper, declare
it the New York City of this morning, even before coffee. Various

states of impermanence are *sine qua non*, fashionable even, when
Versace is shot or St. Laurent retires, dolled up in pastel slacks, like
the dinosaurs, extinct as if they'd donned white belts. Northwest,

I voyage, in the wake of the Celto-Iberians, and a hundred other
human constellations. Literature ennobles us entirely, plots no
Bloom or Frye could get to the deep source of. Me, personally, I run

like a motor till the key stops turning, just because I'm running on sand
like a hermit crab in search of its hole, and largely because
I can. Whatever wild saltations, there's a motel stayed in by somebody

already, Odysseus never had that, I'll bet, turning down the sheets at
Circe's Motor Lodge, to find the slick stains of other men, the shooting
stars of lovers loaded on the bed, like postcards wishing

he was there. I guess everything he did was done on air, like
no one did it before. The earth was young and full of lessons unlearned,
kennings and cursive lines and a poetry young as you'd wish, with

no cliché yet spoken. The whole damn place was reeking with hope, gods
not yet hamstrung, no voice choked with cancer or the learned
hopelessness of ever and ever after. No Ministry of Immigrants

with a visa to stamp or an HIV test to wield like the bolt of Zeus.
No resumé of last lives with testimonials and degrees like those bestowed
by the Order of Oz. No, this was the maiden cruise, and we won't

see the like of it again, as all of us have lived before, and have visas
stamped like tattoos on our lolling baby heads. / April, 19–, wind
NNW, charted avidly by the god of memory. There's a good blow, out

on the whaleroad, threading us among the floes – for days, in fact,
it's been effortless. We're still in the equatorial current, though it's bearing
pack ice. Teddy strums the banjo, turtle with a zest for life, for

sure. Said he played the Savoy, moons back, we were just raving enough
to be credulous. In Teddy's head, musicians entertain us, up from
steerage. Death in the offing. All democratic, says Ted. (Safety alone leads

113

to despots, witness the dead-eyed men who flatten our freedom with
law, because frankly, they have all the time in the world.) Spring
pervades the air. It is a cold peach orchard, so cold. The moon in full

brought flights of wild geese to settle on open water; they're immune to subzero
readings, unconscious of irony, warm innards practicing to be goose liver paté,
wise enough not to know it. I broke out a lined book and wrote

an hour against the desperate sky, as beautiful as I cared to make it: stippled
cloud against Blue, Pantone 2985, like the opening of *The Simpsons*. A designer
drew this cel, through which we animate, lovely lives a smoky hearthwarm

smudge against chill universes, like the black strips between frames. Come
to think, it might as well have been a movie. (Years later, I dangled the rights
in front of a producer, who snuffled it like a hog and brought out his own

film, cadged largely from my book. You can't trust these men with cigars,
orchestrating the farce of other lives with the dim music of their own desires,
shadowmen in front of others' fires, sipping cognac at their clubs

at the back of Plato's cave, off limits to the likes of us....) Now Teddy has
his banjo down in his lap, takes a quaff of whisky, regales us with childhood
tales: *I'm turtle soup in a gilded pot, Teddy's my name and I like it a lot....*

– Coré, you laugh. You know I have reason to fear the sea, its skin
no less than depths, that I laughed until bubbles spiraled from my mouth
and darkness came on me like a hangman's hood....

She wanted me to take the sea back as my own, like getting back
on a bike, & was being typically grandiose and Greek. She'd
kiss the nape of my neck and say, 'Sing, quill,' while the parchment

sky rolled out its noisy fakery and I inscribed
my latest song to her. 'So, here,' I said:

                             He sailed west from Crete
in a newmoon boat, vines wrapped round him, grapes in his mouth. The

vine leaves had fallen by Pharos, scattered by the sea. At next landfall
three nymphs came aboard – harbour inspection, they said – but the stamp
on his passport was the last civil thing. Tiller

lodged beneath an arm, he swigged from a jar, every so
often wiping wine from his chin. Through dark he tossed on cold lees
and his little craft rode the breakers through Hercules' gate.

The wines went north with him, sealed in amphoras with the mark
of Athena. Jars stood between him and Orion like the bars
of a makeshift jail. Wind tipped the sail's cup, an Atlantic gale, often

taking him from land's sight. He thought, This is the winegod's
diaspora....

Okay, Scheherazade, let's stop for a drink. / In reply
a slow grin. She made gin and tonics. We listened to Tom Waits.

I caught glissandos and minor thirds, icicle breeze, sheets of rain.
Started to sing the blues / come home little girl, papa ain't
salty no more. / *You said, 'You're just your young self in its older*

calculations,' but you only understood me when I sang. Talk in prose
and the muse finds an urgent elsewhere, abandons her creation
in a tinkerbell contrail. Don't worry. She'll be back before

we sail.... Stroll off to any meadow; wait. Wait, counting hours on
a daisy chain. My evolved bones hear birdsong. There is a book by a biologist
who says there is no purpose to life, we are just in the world to see; to let

mystery settle into us, before leaving it. Watch long enough and someone will
invent the alto sax, write a novel without vowels, train chimps to
perform it. There will be a series of serial killings. A ploughshare will

sharpen itself into a sword. Rationales will be devised, lest the killings not
have meaning. Some will try original thinking. No one is original, of course – but
gets consequence and cause messed up; no wonder we worship arbitrary

gods; the earth's a magical place thereby, with wrung-neck swans and
grave owls; with thought running like blood in our consciousness, with only
a bootstrap segue into afterlife; a roadmap, a shining negative. Small

time bombers have made the world intolerable for the smug; for
anyone, in fact. Press meaninglessness on solid citizens, you'll see
how they run. Some small particle of thinking, some small human

token, shot at a gas pump, obituary all sized up. As if we needed
reminding of randomness. Isles shake themselves free from the continent, drift
to their locus, like targets in a gallery. Animals and birds range far

and wide, settling with their fortunes to a spot on the wheel, like *Duck Hunt*
on the old Nintendo, to be picked off by natural selection, like all of us, heart
a target of concentric circles, inviting the sniper, harvester

of souls, Jesus gathering all up like bobbing yellow ducks on the river.
Of those I loved, scythed off at the knees, I think now. Stubble in the field.
Geese rose again from the lake this morning, wheeled south,

though autumn is long and gentle, tickling them on the throat as they
sun in the north and dream of taking off; because no place is like that
place, that place you can run to. It is in the fall of the year I travel, at least

in the mind. That the warm wind seems cold, I can't reckon. It must have
to do with the shortness of the day, sun angling low, shattering the leaves
with its brightness, but a dark descending, a dark with owls, so I

abandon all I ever thought was true, all those I swore eternal fealty to, or
simply betrayed. It only takes a single thought of leaving, and I'm gone. Leaving
sunning frogs in their unmoving pond to dream to next spring, when it's

already stuck in their throats. They want a mate now, they want to travel,
though winter ripped their tickets in half, half a month ago, and now lets
summer linger in the rippled water, over which I saw the damselfly, itself

a frayed thread of summer, an ardent heart geared for the circus coupling
these fragile creatures do on their trapeze, putting the earthbound gently
from their dream back to the ground. Okay, all-knowing nature sez, this

is the last sex anyone will ever have, from your point of view anyhow.
face down in the mud, frost coming, the scythe coming, the anthem
some heavy metal theme of a decade past, or more; it's like the nightmare

of that high school tryst, in a narrow back seat, a Fiat or Beetle, training
the avian heart to go down and feel the world on its back, the bones' print
in mud, a library book soon closed, numbered, filed, never

123

borrowed – a big book there as a headstone. Me, I'm thinking of an apple tree, an avalon for my ashes, to say I flew like those ashes fly, willynilly in wind, to settle like a seed, where I may. / Sea songs: *The Owl and the Pussycat*

went to sea. / On champagne, the unsinkable Titanic slid into the Atlantic. / One hundred thirty-four triremes sailed off to Sicily to get wrecked, according to Thucydides. / Columbus sailed the ocean blue. / Tyrannosaurs ambled the North Sea,

when it was a wading pond. / Moses parted the water so chariots could race towards a tryst with modern history, in Palestine, in Two Thousand Two. / The ocean, slumbering, hears deep in a shell the turn of the screw. / Algae

blooms deoxygenize the atmosphere. / On some time scale, these
things little matter, but on the Carolina Banks last summer I let the waters
sweep up over my feet. Crabs frolicked like today was the only day,

cannily husbanding their holes. / That night I read of Scheherazade
of all the nights she borrowed back, until she was a slim Armageddon
of her own, dashing her world to the floor to see it break. Have we made

enough sons and daughters in the soupy tides? Like Teddy's tribe,
and their childish walk to the waves, trusting the currents to carry them from danger.
And back? There is that narrow frame where we can return to the rivers

of our birth. What to do there? Dozens of the aged are playing canasta. They
are conservative, and want to judge. They can barely keep score, Parkinsonian
jellos quivering with righteousness. Careful what you become. / And the young –

in one another's arms, quiverless, without thought. Time's baleen jaws scoop them
by the million, like plankton; tank tops and painted toenails; tattooed arms – no part
of the fossil record, like their poems, about love. / you dance, you don't

dance. Little matters, here in the night, a distance beyond willing. / I dreamt
of depths last night, anxieties, indeterminacies, but the sum was sleep. I cannot say
I feared anything. In fact, as the stars wheeled, I felt a great peace, my bones

outlined against the sky, like girders, an electric arc of an idea,
a blueprint. / Little boat bobbed on the waves, a coracle, blown west on the year's
first hurricane. Basking on dunes as the storm neared, I assumed

no equations extended to the next day. Who knows if that next wave
contains not just the seafood buffet, but a sharkish waiter with a wide
white smile. We like to think our world has us at the centre, as the

crabs do, no doubt, scurrying to black holes in the sand, while
the sea wanders its familiar shore. A sun burned blandly, its physics
known to knowing's horizon: oceans will boil off in a few million

years. Earth will become Mars. Meantime, I don't know if a wave
will engulf my sand ménage – book, towel, sunglasses, chilled beer – and sink
my chair, sucking me out to sea. I postcard myself. I am where I am. No pen

to write; keyboard to key on. No address but the sand. Columbus
washed up south of here. If he'd waited a bit, he could have done it live on
CNN, a man sick with gold and travel. Eating crabcakes, I think

of that colonial fact, with white wine, with no serious care.
My body pale and imperial, heart beating, waiting for the gold of resolution,
working on my tan. / *Back home, checking the mail. Most everyone who needs*

cash has my address; apparently 'Milky Way Galaxy' was not vague enough for the marketeers. Forced now to consider I am not on a beach, not sailing blue oceans, not hunting the Islands of Ash. All those years getting home-

sick postings from Ted, in Athens, Paris, Bali, everywhere the warm salt tide took him, while I sailed the fields, harrowed golden seas, grew as close and familiar to the earth as the weeds and flowers. Had, by my own

count, five and a half lives, eight houses, herculean amounts of wine, some made with my own grapes. Six ex-lovers I afterwards kept track of, many more at addresses I could not memorize or wanted to forget. They fight over

space in the bed, are that smoky smell in the wood, in the house where each
one was. Perhaps the house I have now is most like a boat, odd-angled planks, darkened
drawers, fitted and invisible cabinets, even a windowed corner that is like a prow,

heaving up on the frozen, fallen grass, which tumbles then down a ravine,
scrawled on by fallen spruce and birch, scribbled with fern and lank wood-edged
grass, then a dark creekside where carnivorous pitcher plants trap fly-bys with

homemade honey. Maybe that is why. I am at sea.

Meantime, clouds pile
high, condominiums of air, zoomed through by 737s, their contrails shaking
thunder out; signs of displeasure in some small-minded god, piqued

by threadbare and picayune sacrifice, now on a petty warpath. Jack
meant to sell the farm, but even after leaving, could not; instead, letting
friend after friend use the place. More books written there than can be

counted, under the enchantment of the old ghost owl. Still, as Ted tap-
dances through his dreams at night and mice scuttle in invisible walls, he's
home half the time, an unbalance understood by none. They would not want

him to go there in his head. So there he went.

V
The Winegod's Diaspora

Coré had me steer north
north-west, by the stars, and correct from time to time, holding close to the headlands
if possible, but not too close, in case the surf should

take us on the rocks. Landfall here would lock us down
until the winds changed, but if we crossed the channel after dark, we might
make it to her father's place, in the unlikely dream

world of sun, lounge chairs and smuggled wine. (In this
same future, Coré has a way of taking me in wide-eyed, as
though settling on a way to be, with me, that in old

ages was already an antique way. Easy to place her
at the fall, or flood, or in the muses' company.) So I continue,
out of sight of land, building sandcastles like those

132

I built on Weymouth sands, in 1953. I still have the photograph, torn
then reassembled, flecks of silver nitrate telling a passing and fragile
tale, halfway finished the moment it began. In the background, two

women walking, long skirts flared at the hip, nipped at the calf,
headscarves, (it's windy), high heels. /
                                    Coré checked the casks
every hour or so, making sure they hadn't shifted. Drink as ballast –

at least until we drank it, or unshipped it and got our pay.
Ideally I would not break the law, not so extravagantly. But this
was easy money, cheap wine from Crete, rebottled for a colder

133

island. For this I was willing to ride the sea, if not go under her
to be trapped in swirling blue skirts of bubbles, out of my mouth with
bubble words inside. (I cannot dive any more. I would have to drink

first.) I tried to make all my fears sit high where I could see them,
at the top end of consciousness; mulling while hauling on that bootstrap
like a halyard. It always was a puzzle – what becomes of thought

after it is thought; of those delicate wavelets of energy. Right now,
port agents look capable of reading my mind. I feel as if I were running
guns, or Afghan opium, instead of a few thousand litres of Minoan

red. Coré reads to me to pass the time: *The bow-shaped boat is ready for the wind, for the north and west, far from the gods' sight. It is known that when the geese fly north, bearing the soul of a king, no mortal*

will live for long. So Dionysus is gone, lies drunk in the Apple Isles perhaps, salacious head in some mortal's lap. In his head the dry, sunny slopes of the vineyard still hold summer heat. The stars are different here, higher

or lower in the sky, though little changed are the soft hands of darkness. The wine jars are stowed in a small turf house.... "We are as lost here," says Coré, "as he, far from his hearth's gods."

/ Those land-

scapes most human are those without us: canyonlands; the salt
beds of old seas; a red ridge edging into the Martian sky. There our
wishes settle in unknown patterns, like

and unlike what they were when they still lived
in us. You have to let them go, not keep them encased
in flesh and bone. Shadows accumulate in the rocky lees

as the sun dogs them, impossible to follow, till they fall
from the edge of the earth. The trail back might once have led
to water, is crooked in ways my heart recognizes. "Before

I fall asleep tonight," I tell Coré, "I am going to think only
of the desert, of a path that once followed flowing water, of a water-
less, red plateau."

                   (How will you get me back to the farm

now that I'm on the North Sea? Wanton lands, broken horizons,
grass growing green, fern explosion, with jewel weed and a lonesome
phoebe, building a nest on my porch. In this restless vision, I think

of myself as the *pro tem locus*, around which everything revolves,
and this is surely the lesson of evolution, with its accident consciousness
bringing all around it into focus, so the welling of life

has someone to see it, and say how it is, and bring the lyric
thought to it, as if I was all here and all the moment, and could
make a poem on it.) Like and unlike our sky; shadows

on the east ridge; a long trail that once might have led
to water, crooked as memory. If a voice comes as it comes
sometimes, it is all I can do to not pick up

the phone, to hear a voice breathing in some other place, unstained
by this. Hello? Another body in my arms, relaying the voice. Her breath
goes sleepy, then near wakefulness, then slow

and deep again, so the voice is reduced
to murmur, the words to waves, thick
and green in the water, and then

to a shimmer far off on the surface; we lie
like weed in water, eye sockets full
of pale light. There is no moon; it comes

from inside.
            Buddy Ebsen came to me
last night in a dream, not as patriarch
of *The Beverly Hillbillies*, but as Davey

Crockett's sidekick from the fifties, younger than Jed, more
of the dancer in him, but ancient wisdom in his eyes, slow
voice, a god's, the same cornpone sentiments as God. He said

thou shalt not, and the rage was clear. Buddy could tower
like the old Greeks, pyrotechnical in his godhead. Then Elly May
interceded for me, falling to her knees, embracing mine, and

ruining all the unities. Then when I awoke it was Coré, herself
semi-divine, but with the modest claim of a bard, going around,
collecting stories. I ask where I am. Her every answer is another

140

question. In exile, everywhere's the same.

A letter to Coré

in London: *the weeds are winning, finally. Trees throw off seedlings, needing
only to grow to the height of my thumb to have a chance. Most will not reach*

*maturity, though one or two will live to provide shade. In my travels
this summer I was most of the time in smoke, blown clear to the Appalachians
from forest fires in Montana and Colorado. It was like being eaten. I swept*

*over the teeth of the Rockies into the belly of a Kansas plain, lost
in a haze of memory. I dreamt at night in chain motels, dreaming
of eating and being eaten, without prejudice. One night*

I dreamt of a trip by boat downriver, to some port, some
ocean, where boats were being offloaded, bobbing empty at the dock
like seedpods. Then they were blessed by charlatans and sent off

to plunder, never to be heard of in god's earth again. Then the galaxies
got swallowed up like spit. I realized the gods were home once more,
quarreling, earthly experiment over, busy slashing each other, neck

to navel, over dice games and store-window mannequins. At the end
of the universe I was left asleep. All I heard was a voice, reading
a Rilke poem. words starting low, staying

low, but building like taste, like breath, until the town forms brown
on the hill's shoulder, and the moon shudders into motion, left
to right. I close my eyes; the page rises from a mouth like speech. It is

not day or night, but like a translation of a galaxy forming.
It makes me think of two fingers resting on a throat, the thrill
of hearing someone write, out loud, when the world was still

forming. The words go on forever for all I know; impossible to tell
where sound ends and sight starts and words fail; only
a light pulse, and breath.

Sometimes I think this of Coré: there may

now be another body in her arms. Dionysus the rum-runner, she
called me, her north world gangland boss, outgunned by no-one
on the high seas, making even Poseidon all smiles and waves.

Her eye sockets brimmed with hoarded light, light from the south where
wine gods come from, to live implausibly on northern hardscrabble. Something
made her come up to me in the Cretan market, strike up talk. When

you talked to her, it was as if you'd dropped a pebble down a deep well; you
wouldn't hear the splash.

                           (At the foot of the Sphinx my dad posed in Arab robes.
He was young, his smile caught by a local photographer; he peered slightly

left, seeing something beyond the frame. I refuse to think
of memory as nostalgia. I think it is consideration. Even the memory
of love has its counters: gametes on a string, or beads

on an abacus. I would have liked to have been a mathematician, hanging
off the rational frame, my head full in the incoherence; the place
I write in, its fathomless depths seen from the other side....)

                                                     And giving

due to the amphibian half of the dance team, a love song by
Ted: *The shell's a fine and private place / but none I think do
there embrace....* He smiles at his own honied words while

the audience waits foolishly on its folding chairs, uncertain whether
the show's over? Ready, Teddy! / But, still singing, the turtle
has sloped off. Could it be he's readying to return to his Sargasso

birthplace, to his own only homely beach, the only one of his
sisters and brothers left, after seven years of carnage at sea? Now, though less
light on his feet and definitely off-Broadway, the good thing is (we

can all say this with the same sense of relief) Ted's too large
a mouthful for anything to eat. In retrospect, those three-martini lunches
at Sardi's might have been, the gossip has it, what saved his

life. So now it's back to sea. Little wonder he turned turtle
in the end, as reprise dips his knees in the Spanish Main: good to be on the open
whaleroad / splish-splash / 'member when you was belly-gashed in

a barfight? with that swordfish bill? / no doubt I hung with tavern scum – my
friend Melville said, "Ruin itself can work little more upon them." / piano rolls
of memory, rolled tight inside this airy skull. / remember that biologist at Sardi's,

who said, "If you want your DNA to be predictable enough to keep you alive,
it must be predictable enough to kill you?" One Faustian bargain, that; another,
wax wings to bear you from a prose-dull land; the long feathered

fall to oblivion. (Ted's late anarchist club and thrash band, *Amphibians
for Oblivion*, succeeded in neither line of work. The motto of both borrowed from
Robert Scholes and screamed at highest volume with Captain Beefheart guitar

pyrotechnics: "We will bestow the name of literature only upon those texts that displace
intention sufficiently to require exegesis.") Whereupon, Jack shifts in his raiments,
startled. The moon, a peach upon two inches of new snow, sails behind cloud to a place

ordained, a ceiling bulb to light him up, warmer a bit than absolute zero, screwed
into the black sky. If it is so cold, why are the glaciers crumbling? He strives
to keep the song in his head, no song he knows, but twisted strings of melody

at harmonic intervals: still the hum of birth and death, the argent moon
above him like the little lightbulb of a cartoon idea, the cartoon of his sacred
sense. Putting on snowshoes and a jacket, he essays out into night, tracking

the deer, wishing he could follow geese, rising from half-frozen bays
to head where open water is. The swamp is frozen into solidness, no
flowing rill, no sign of where the pitcher plant trapped flies in its honeyed

seas, where once pampas grass and green ferns grew higher than
your head, and now frozen to a flat, featureless tundra. Rules don't
hold sway. Ontogeny does not recapitulate phylogeny. The air

holds zero water, zero heat. Ice makes the going easier. You can almost skate.
The woods are open, accessible. (Love's letter lost: you had me on fast forward
a year, unable to revisit what I'd said I'd said; and you know what I do best is

consider. I'd said to you, it was all passionately present, as we are taught
the best love is. But I don't believe it – that love is a giving in. Even lust
has its counters, glissandic beads slid left to right in sum, as if it could be

toted by an abacus. I'd said I would have liked it if you had been
a mathematician, sliding into incoherence precisely because of the rational
ideal you clung to, trying to trim the sail in a gale-force wind. Let those

winds howl in you, answering the howl inside, but let you count them, answer
the symmetry, and cry for that…. I'd said maybe my fault is I always knew
my medium: on the skin of the earth, ducking to breathe the air that glanced

off into maelstroms of solar wind, spinning in a hide coracle, or, as now, in this
wineboat, taking viniculture north and west. I am always on an edge. If you
inhabit a medium too deeply, you are lost in it, your life a matchhead, swelling

to light a fire. Didn't all life on land dwell on that edge once, neither
shore nor sea? Back and forth, the texts so indeterminate, the language less
than less? Tide swell was then a mother's song, lulling to both sleep

and waking, the dream between, a strand littered with little crab claws, perfectly nihilistic as signposts of life. Now we squirm into sarcophagal positions, every word screaming *eat me, bury me, scatter me*, and every so often, *read this poem*.

I'd said I was both hearthfire and holocaust, & I was only speaking for myself. I am only speaking.) Q: you tried to go back out, out to sea again. A: that's pretty obvious. Q: why, if you were afraid of the deeps, did you

keep living on the surface – of the sea, I mean? A: I was looking at the break-through, but I grew enamored of the breakers, of life at the brink. The brink of the drink – I sailed there. Q: you took up

sailing. A: it passed the time. O, a life on the ocean wave. Q: and did you think
what lay so many fathoms down? A: I drew word pictures of it, by
the fathom. I sold it all to magazines, the words. I let my fears be

buoyed up by the tales I told, so they would never sink. Q: but now
and then you must have thought – how shall I put it – thought
of Davey Jones' locker down there? A: there was no down there, down there,

to borrow a line of Gertrude Stein. Q: that's over my head. A: and
won't leave mine....
       Darwin: "For in the larger country there will
have existed more individuals, and more diversified forms,

and the competition will have been severer, and thus the standard
will have been rendered higher." (It never said, on the box of poison, that
if I killed those mice, eating my house piecemeal, that I'd be left

with the hopeless squeaking of babies, abandoned by a nasty death.
I had steeled myself against the nasty death, but not against the
shivering high cries. My karmic share is less tonight, and I stumble against

the darkness, my heart beating wildly, oxygen poisoning me,
with a life still half to go that is one mistake after another, and no
wisdom to hoard like unassayed ore, and utter with shiny

spoken pebbles, and with no tears that can be honestly shed.)

As I write this
I am second last in a line of bipedal apes; that is, I have a daughter, last
in line so far. And as we walked hand in hand one time way back, I thought of

how we'd separated from the pack, were off alone, as even longer back some others
must have done in the Alps or Olduvai, bored with just chipping flint; bored
with the dislocated haunch of something run down and cornered and killed,

no poem or grace said on its head, and served cold as Gertrude's wedding
feast, spiceless and bloody; bored with the tribe's bourgeois righteousness.
What I am dining on now comes from a package and might be genetically

altered, which we all are come to think of it, when we're spun
out of two others. Those mortal coils are prescient, and a sight longer lived
than us. Two to tango, two to build a whole new double helix; two to unwind

themselves and coil anew together. And this is no stronger
or better, just newer than the two (and knows it all). Now: I am
camping in a brick-walled loft on Notre-Dame, sat by a fireplace for which

nature has neglected to provide trees. So it's cold. I am sipping
old scotch (half as old as me). I am too old to want to go back on the sea
but the calls won't relent from the Sirens' island, from the throats

of birdwomen, from places undiscovered that I tried to shuck the
known for. I said to my daughter I wanted her to look at sundown
on a headland no one ever saw: in the end, I said, that's what Eric

had Leif for. What Snorri sang so bittersweet about, when the Northmen
went out. With hat and cane, I'm waiting in the wings for the right *doowop*,
my cue. On the tin roof a steady rain, in whose puddles who knows what will

grow, because who knows what was sown. Teddy picks up his gilded pot, etched
with grave commonplace like a pharaoh's tomb, his own story weighing him
down, an anchor and sarcophagus. So off he sets in the ocean sea, bottled

message for anyone to read & solve the shell game. *The shell's a fine and private place.*

Now, the plane of orbits & yearly drift
have lined five planets up like duck pins, to be bowled over – if you

imagine them on their way you'll think too fast. No cataclysm moves
as slow as their wanderings. A star blowing up takes lifetimes
to see. Long enough to write the elegy. We are almost at midpoint of

world's end; its emblems any seven things we choose, its numbers full of meaning
for the devout: one muse, two minds, three-four time – a waltz – five books, one
hundred fifty-eight sections, four hundred seventy-two stanzas, one thousand

158

four hundred fourteen lines, tap-

dancing one half exit line, the hook.